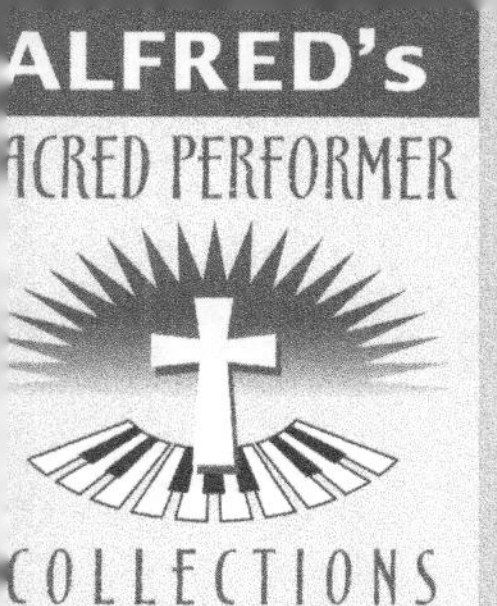

NCED PIANO

Medleys *for* Blen… Christmas

10 Contemporary Arrangements of Praise Songs with Carols

Arranged by Carol Tornquist

Traditional carols are often performed alongside contemporary Christmas songs in many of today's church services, giving rise to the term *blended worship.* This distinctive collection provides a valuable resource for pianists who want to play familiar holiday tunes in a tasteful and new style in addition to current Christmas songs of praise recognizable to most congregations.

In order to help the traditional and contemporary songs flow together, I have incorporated new harmonies, meters, and rhythmic patterns in the carols so that both songs become one piece of music. Even though each medley is complete in itself, I have also created the option of playing from one arrangement to the next when a longer solo is needed. "Segue" is marked at the end of each arrangement, meaning an easy transition from one medley to the next is possible since the new key will be compatible with the previous one.

May these new settings of timeless Christmas melodies, although composed centuries apart, enhance the worship experience for you and your listeners.

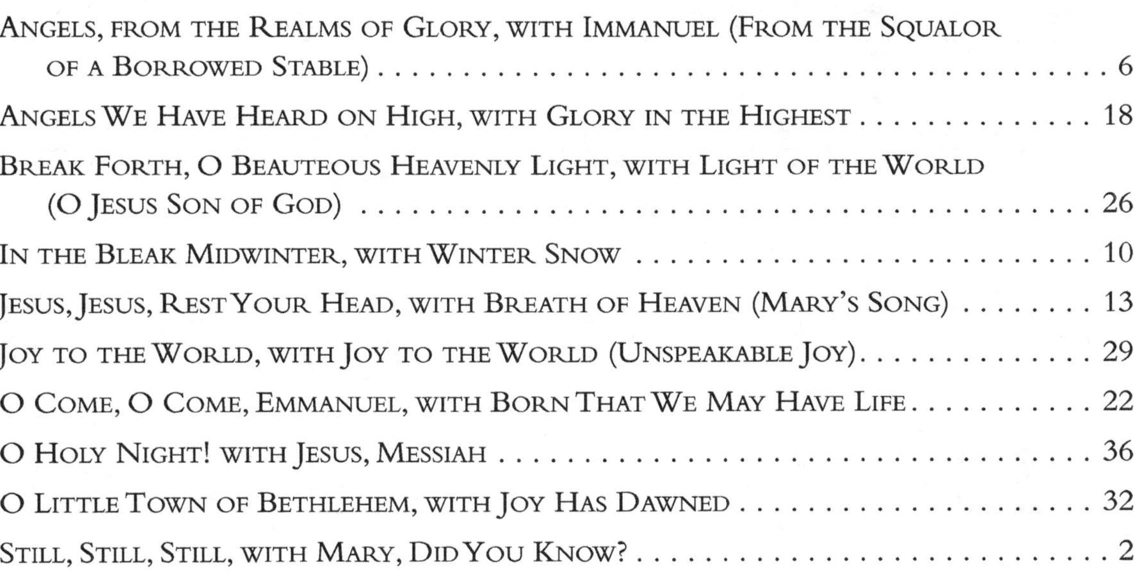

Angels, from the Realms of Glory, with Immanuel (From the Squalor of a Borrowed Stable) 6

Angels We Have Heard on High, with Glory in the Highest 18

Break Forth, O Beauteous Heavenly Light, with Light of the World (O Jesus Son of God) 26

In the Bleak Midwinter, with Winter Snow 10

Jesus, Jesus, Rest Your Head, with Breath of Heaven (Mary's Song) 13

Joy to the World, with Joy to the World (Unspeakable Joy) 29

O Come, O Come, Emmanuel, with Born That We May Have Life 22

O Holy Night! with Jesus, Messiah 36

O Little Town of Bethlehem, with Joy Has Dawned 32

Still, Still, Still, with Mary, Did You Know? 2

Produced by
Alfred Music Publishing Co., Inc.
P.O. Box 10003
Van Nuys, CA 91410-0003
alfred.com

Printed in USA.

ISBN-10: 0-7390-7318-4
ISBN-13: 978-0-7390-7318-6

Cover Photos
Mary and Jesus: © istockphoto / hisks • Poinsettia: © istockphoto / Tfawls

(Approx. Performance Time – 3:45)

Still, Still, Still
with
Mary, Did You Know?

Arr. Carol Tornquist

"Mary, Did You Know?"
Words and Music by Mark Lowry and Buddy Greene
a tempo
p
mp

41
45
49
53
58
mf molto rit.

63
a tempo
mp
5
67
1
71
2
4
75
cresc.
2
80
mf
4
2
1
molto rit.
p
(segue)

(Approx. Performance Time – 2:00)

Angels, from the Realms of Glory
with
Immanuel
(From the Squalor of a Borrowed Stable)

Moderately, in two (𝅗𝅥 = 69)

"Angels, from the Realms of Glory"
Words by James Montgomery
Music by Henry T. Smart

Arr. Carol Tornquist

17
cresc.
mf
21
dim.
"Immanuel (From the Squalor of a Borrowed Stable)"
Words and Music by Stuart Townend
1 2 1
mp
25
28
mf
5
31
5
1

35
39
5
5
3
1
dim.
2
1
43
3
3
mp
47
3
5
2
4
51
1

55
5
2
p
59
62
65
69
2
1
2
1
mp molto rit.
1
(segue)

(Approx. Performance Time – 3:15)

In the Bleak Midwinter
with
Winter Snow

Hushed and unhurried, like falling snow (♩ = 80)

Arr. Carol Tornquist

"In the Bleak Midwinter"
Words by Christina Rossetti
Music by Gustav Holst

mp

rit.

pedal ad lib.

4

a tempo

13
2
4
16
mf
5
3
3
19
a tempo
rit.
mp
1
22
p rit.
4
"Winter Snow"
Words and Music by Audrey Assad
a tempo
25
5
3
2
mp
4
5
2
1
3

28
31
mf
34
a tempo
poco rit.
37
1.
dim.
41
2.
mp
rit.
p
(segue)

Jesus, Jesus, Rest Your Head
with
Breath of Heaven (Mary's Song)

Arr. Carol Tornquist

16
More movement
poco rit.
mp
20
23
poco rit.
26
Tempo I
p
30
poco rit.

Moderately slow, in two
"Breath of Heaven (Mary's Song)"
Words and Music by Amy Grant and Chris Eaton
34
mp
38
42
mf
46
50

53
3
poco rit.
a tempo
mp
56
59
4
2
5
1
poco rit.
62
a tempo
3
2
5
65
2
4
2
1
poco rit.

68
a tempo
72
poco rit.
76
a tempo
p
80
84
Freely
mp
pp
(segue)

(Approx. Performance Time – 2:15)

Angels We Have Heard on High
with
Glory in the Highest

"Glory in the Highest"
Words and Music by Ed Cash, Chris Tomlin, Jesse Reeves, Daniel Carson and Matt Redman

32
36
40
44
4
3
1
mf
2
48

52
rit.
56
Broadly
5
f
59
3
3
63
3
67
ff
f
(segue)

(Approx. Performance Time – 2:15)

O Come, O Come, Emmanuel
with
Born That We May Have Life

Slowly, in two (𝅗𝅥 = 58)

"O Come, O Come, Emmanuel"
Latin hymn
Plainsong, adapted by Thomas Helmore

Arr. Carol Tornquist

16
rit.
a tempo
20
24
rit.
27
Broadly
f
30

"Born That We May Have Life"
Words and Music by Ed Cash, Chris Tomlin and Matt Maher

45
mf
2
48
51
3
1
5
54
1
3
rit.
57
p
8va
(segue)

(Approx. Performance Time – 3:30)

Break Forth, O Beauteous Heavenly Light
with
Light of the World (O Jesus Son of God)

Slowly and steadily (♩ = 72)

"Break Forth, O Beauteous Heavenly Light"
Words by Johann Rist
Music by Johann Schop

Arr. Carol Tornquist

20
a tempo
molto rit.
mp
24
a tempo
molto rit.
28
"Light of the World (O Jesus Son of God)"
Words and Music by Matt Redman
31
34

37
mf
41
45
49
1.
53
2.
mp
molto rit.
(segue)

JOY TO THE WORLD
with
JOY TO THE WORLD (UNSPEAKABLE JOY)

Moderately, with confidence (♩ = 126)

Arr. Carol Tornquist

"Joy to the World"
Words by Isaac Watts
Music by G. F. Handel

21
cresc.
f
25
5
mf
5
3
1
29
33
3
37
cresc.
4
3
1
f
2

"Joy to the World (Unspeakable Joy)"
Arrangement and additional chorus by Ed Cash, Matt Gilder and Chris Tomlin

(Approx. Performance Time – 3:00)

O Little Town of Bethlehem
with
Joy Has Dawned

14
17
a tempo
mp rit.
rit.
20
Steadily
"Joy Has Dawned"
Words and Music by Keith Getty and Stuart Townend
mf
23
26

29
32
35
a tempo
rit.
38
41

44
47
a tempo
rit.
50
rit.
mp
53
a tempo
cresc.
f
rit. e dim.
56
p
(segue)

(Approx. Performance Time – 3:30)

O Holy Night!
with
Jesus, Messiah

Arr. Carol Tornquist

17
21
4
25
2
3
4
poco rit.
29
a tempo
3
2
33
2
3
cresc.
molto rit.

37
a tempo
mf
41
45
49
5
4
2
2
53
f
1

56
a tempo
molto rit.
mf
60
molto rit.
Moderately
"Jesus, Messiah"
Words and Music by Daniel Carson,
Chris Tomlin, Ed Cash and Jesse Reeves
63
mp
67
71

74
mf
3
5
78
3
molto rit.
4
82
Broadly
f
3
3
3
2
86
3
molto rit.
5
90
ff
8va